A Sky Full of Str

Olga Dermott-Bond

Published by Nine Pens

2021

www.ninepens.co.uk

ISBN: 978-1-8384321-2-6

003

For my sister, Esther

Contents:

"In the burned house I am eating breakfast.
You understand: there is no house, there is no breakfast,
Yet here I am"

Margaret Atwood
Morning in the burned house

Oíche na Goithe Móire

The night of the big wind, Ireland, 1839

You don't believe me when I tell you
some of my children flew away, bodies
scattered far, first found by crows,
shaken from their cauldron nests. You don't
believe me when I tell you I stumbled over
broken bones of branches, when I sing
of the dead shaking loose from their graves,
each body sifted through shallow soil.

You don't believe my eyes stared at a sky full
of strange specimens. The awful darkness.
Have I told you how the moon lay on her back,
full to the brim of great lakes? Have you heard
how the air bent beneath heavy emptiness so still,
I could hear the whispers between walls of farmhouses?
I tell you, again, the priests wept inside churches
with no roofs, prayed while the skin of the earth

split open. You don't believe me, but I tell you,
I could not have dreamt such a night as this.

Miscarriage

It must have been a boy. Ten days late –
        my heart turned to soft coral
swaying in ferocious heat of bath water.

Weighted pain of his quietness, then this –
        sail torn and unstitched, sinking slowly
        below my bloodied thighs, and blackened

bladderwrack floating across the surface.
        I dredged the fine threads as best I could
until I held a limp curl of seahorses in my hand –

I turned off the bathroom light, lay so still
        on the seabed, hearing each uneasy muscle
        of pulse under shallows of my skin, pelvis picked

white, ribbons of flesh floating to feed
        angelfish, bath gritty with salt and sand, one
less pearl to count.

31 Green Lane

The day we moved in, Pearl and Claude left
late-summer sweet pea wrapped in damp
newspaper on the doorstep. Tanya had opened
the windows wide all day, so the outside

was on the inside; bees slept on windowsills,
ladybirds gossiped in the pantry. No deadlock,
gas fire like a broken trolley, creaking cistern,
woodchip, arthritic stair carpet, phantom cat smell, tired lino.

A trust exercise with no furniture, just a bed
borrowed from his parents' pub; the divan's
two strangely light halves held together
by clasps like tiny crotchets. I remember only

an idling of poppies, swayed by the opera
of roses that gathered around our back door,
singing to wildness that, later, would make my dad
despair. No fear yet of woodrot, convolvulus, ivy.

Miss Havisham lies awake the night before her wedding

Slipped from her stays, the sun sighs slowly past
my room. Honeyed midsummer lulls, leans back
lazily, so I can keep vigil over this last
night of girlhood. My dolls' faces are cracked
with envy; I think of dust that will gather
in their blind eyes. I will forget them. Undressed,
taken between his sheets, I will tremble, eager
to take sin from its pulpit, my skin caressed
until this marble body is moulded far
from mother's silence, daughter's duty. "Thou
Shalt Not" will be stained red, breathless, our laughter
making servants blush before breakfast, their wonder
at our happiness. One last singling twilight;
my nectared blood. Love hums fearless, bright.

Upside down girl

Portrait of Anne Bonny

Squatting in the kitchen, she caught me,
slippery little sea urchin. Ma always
told me I came from the end of the world,
dangling from the end of a black rope.

Kinsale. I remember leftovers for tea,
pendulum of master's footsteps upstairs,
my blood his echo. Downstairs, Ma's bruised
apron, knuckles like blackberries. Always

rain. My first night on open sea I laughed
in narrow darkness, dreamt of cutting
men open and rubies tumbling out, eyes
blind like gold coins. I know how water

will rot the finest velvet, swallow silver
whole, but this place brings yellowthroats,
woodstars, nights filled with naked heat,
dry scrape of crickets. I have stolen a ship

to keep the world away and lie on her
deck in the darkness, feeling my unborn
swim towards me, his two fists fierce
as rocks hidden underneath this place.

Mother, somehow

Lungs full of thunderstorm, curled on the cot floor,
length of a leveret, spine curved with all
your unlearnt languages, star dust formed into
floating acorn fists. I studied your skull,
fresh-sprung forest seamed with silk thread; bight
of thigh, bone-supple body traced to feet
like rubbed pennies. Minute heart cockled tight,
swimming fast with your first teaspoon of milk-sleep.

But there was fear in those first mosaic of hours;
the night seemed brittle against your plum cheek
when I brought you home, my body drowned
with metallic pain, nerves like flint, each fleck
of breath counted as rain on the window –
you on the outside now. Me your mother, somehow.

Before Depakote

i.

our kitchen oiled blue and swaying, tilted by the smell
of his full glass, the second or third if I get home too

late, music full-volume-ugly talking talking talking.
no sleep for weeks on end –

ii.

parked on the bridge over the a46, the road beneath
black water, he wants to unfasten his seatbelt, watch

himself swim through air in silhouette, both daughters
in the backseat, tired faces like new moons rising –

iii.

bath time. stripy frog and baby penguin lie capsized on
the seabed, I squeeze rubber ducks that must be rotting

inside and wait for him. night-stranded quiet folds in
on itself, fear feathered tight against my ribs –

Olga, we thought you'd like to see this memory from 8 years ago

Sky like cough syrup, her smile is snow, doesn't know weight of rock, ice, roots, earth. Search for the fracture that started it all, but it's hidden beneath that coat she loved – she's not struggling yet, doesn't know soon, she'll be buried up to the neck. I want to shake this girl, peel her naked, tell her she won't be able to swim out; an ice cube in his gin cracking still enough to send her falling, suffocated, somewhere she won't be able to reach –

Declaration

The Golden Shovel

*"You'll never ease
The grieving of worms. The mushrooms build their
bookshelves where birch bark used to be."*

'Churchgoing' by Trent

You text me and ask me *how I am*. I hesitate. You'll
never know how difficult this is, because I can never
speak of *once upon a time* again; I've lost the painful ease
of my unhappily ever after that I couldn't hide from you. The
reply I give is a lie. *I'm OK (ish)*. It hides this wolf, a grieving
that prowls long and late. I want to tell you the *ish* consists of
a hard floor of pecked breadcrumbs, of gritted nights, worms
crawling blind between pale ribs, slowly decomposing the
hope I allowed to spore and bloom into deadly mushrooms
which are the only things I want to eat. Starving, I try to build
a shelter with parenthesis, walls that can't meet, their
dark space, making me stoop. I want you to find bookshelves
of confessions that I haven't written yet, those spaces where
I have torn away pages, naked, damp-mottled, stripped birch
blank, because stories are scratched into the farthest bark
of this place I know you will never find, my fingers used
to send a protest, a dark flare, a trail of stones, a declaration to
let you know I am still lost, not knowing how to be.

raining somewhere else

i sometimes think that everything that has ever happened to
me
is raining somewhere else. i sometimes think that the water
has found
a path through high trees, worked a way inside another room,
so the damp
next door is spreading, curving an unknown ceiling into a
misshapen moon.
i sometimes think that if i find that moon, her distended face
will stretch,
mouth sob open, her grey tears gaping for something else. i
sometimes think
that every sky will blister like a dead paint, flake between my
fingers. i
sometimes think of the years minutes months days that i have
stood outside
 arms stretched, hair flattened like dead leaves, skin
unstitched, holding out
a cracked glass, trying to catch everything that has ever
happened to me.

mouthguard

to be forty three and have to grope quietly
in the dark through the confusion
of my bedside table for its ugly grey plastic –
a bad second-hand joke, a contusion
shaped like the inside of my mouth, wet fossil
of bad dreams, half swallowed, half stuck.

to know that some mornings it will have
escaped, crawling like a crustacean across the fine-
sands of mum's illness, ground down by our silence.
half-sleep settles and weighs on my jawline,
my mouth a midnight pumpkin turned into lead,
teeth as seeds hard-pressed, on edge, ready to spit.

What I mean when I say I know a hawk from a handsaw

After Eve L. Ewing

I mean the sun was in my eyes for too long,
each wall a washed out headache when I went

back inside, my room buried in damp-soil-quiet.
I mean I had glimpsed myself for a moment,

high above the earth, my body ruthless, expectant
so much of my energy and strength to stay where

I was, watching, still watching from a distance,
blown like ocean waves of wheat billowing

in high summer while I circled, strained –
I mean it was like finding a feather, feeling

its sieved-flour softness against my fingers,
oiled lightness of something that had flown,

its flimsy strength ancient, primal, a warning.
I mean how easy it was to sense a closeness

hovering over my skin, a thin-milked arrow,
an opaque muteness that had been shot too far,

until it stammered and flinched in a wet tangle-
heavy weave, that couldn't be straightened out

afterwards. I mean I had caught myself between
fickering hedges, smaller than you would think

and not so easily tamed, a creature that didn't
understand all there was left was a stomach full

of stones. I mean there is a tiny part that can't
ever be caught, the trick of your absence a hood

that has turned my heart into sudden night.

Chitengelo

She heard the men's cry first –
Mayi – ba - ba – b - e - e - e
St George's hospital suddenly
brimful of this oil-and-ribbon sound,

something from the very depth
of their being, windows slick with
this new darkness. Then the women –
ye – e – e - e - e – egh, a tender

duskiness that reached the bones
at the Cemetery on Blackshaw Road,
making the foxes turn their heads
from damp soil in back gardens.

She stood stock still, caught between
the too-thin blue curtain, the next
narrow bed; an ancient river humming
and running through her spine.

She wished she could have cried
that *chitengelo* at the end, after
weeks of quiet fury, sitting with her mum,
once a bed had been brought downstairs,

creeping to take turns with her brother,
dad, watching her lie at the bottom
of a lake, eyes closed, her beloved birds
building their nests again in the garden.

For Jenny

'The walls of the house fold themselves down
And the house turns
Itself inside out, as a tulip does
In its last full blown moment'

Margaret Atwood

Mrs Florence Skelton's house falls into the sea, 1946

The last thing I remember
was the kettle calling.

I had always loved being
high over cliffs, waves

crumpling like rock, paper,
scissors. Coming back from

the kitchen, there was a great
haul of wind and the living room

swayed like a drunk man,
the door splayed on its hinges,

until the lintel hung
like a broken elbow.

Cup in hand, I edged forward
as the walls dissolved

into the black bible of sea
like the spoon of sugar in my tea.

Tyrella Beach, July 1979

"And we're all owed joy/ sooner or later /The trick's to remember
whenever/ It was or to see it coming."

Carol Ann Duffy

I promise that nothing bad
is going to happen in this poem,
and unlike the other holidays
we wrote afterwards, we're all happy.

Me, my sister and my mum driving
in our yellow car to July, 1979.
The sooner we get to Aunty Gwen's
caravan the better, brown sofa (or bed

if it's night), purple smell of lit gas,
whistling kettle, fat chips scribbled
in vinegar. Uncle Walter's binoculars
are the heavy kind; blur of a gull

sharpened by its call. Careful –
the trick's to hopscotch now
in sandals from one narrow slat
of wood to another without falling

into soft sink of dune path. Orange
trim of my swimsuit, sand in my bum

shivering when it dries, Esther's
concentration, tapping an upturned

bucket like it might disappear or
talk back, freckles like syrup speckles.
This is a poem about the kite-lightness
a day can bring, or the weight of absence

once it's over – but no, nothing bad
is going to happen in this poem,
because I'm still running
towards the waves, still see

mum's turquoise dress, lilac
mountains, smell of Uvistat; still feel
the tangle of sheets in a strange-safe
bed, promise of the next day coming.

Dragonfly

Scintilla of rain   stitched together

           I find an empress   on my ceiling

        Body of a hair's breadth   wings

    of silk borrowed from a   spider's web.

      Together   we try out to work out why

     the world has fallen flat   she pushes

against the ceiling   traps of painted

          corners.   Beauty's gentle punishment

living only as long   as these lockdown

   months.   I coax her into the broad light

      ask her to fly   backwards, untangle our

too-many mistakes.   She asks nothing   from me

     hums as she hovers   in emerald, flitting

   to sew up   the fissured sky over my head.

Tigress

We watch a programme about stray
animals being rescued. I have to look
away. A kitten, head perfect like a penny,

has stilled herself with a mute suffering
of burnt cork bulging black where her left
eye should be. I learn that there are beautiful

names for rotten things. Necrosis. Ischemia.
I realise that she is better half blind, almost
beautiful again, a tigress both before and after,

right eye and all claws ready.

Working from home

i.

I watch the neighbour's cat, back slung low like a hammock, balancing
an equation of a bird in a hedge. Inside, altars of laptops, half the world
undressed from waist down, bent neck, stiff shoulders. Sunlight lulls

ii.

my tired skin with leaf stencil, drags untidy roses against glass, while
dust motes protest in silence, falling into the still pond of my screen.
A champagne froth of flies fizz over slow-trickling afternoon, until

iii.

crows are loosened in an amber orchard, clouds gather in bright prayer,
trees bare themselves, black magnets to draw calls close. An older face
caught frowning yet again in grey light, disciple to godless lists beneath

my fingertips, body and crooked blood.

Biology homework

Still some red in her hair, my mum took me down
to the lough edge, always at home with leftovers

of empty shells, translating how they had once
lived, turning over unnoticed millennia in her hands.

Late August afternoon, Strangford cold hollowing
my back as we leant over pools, I was a reluctant

student, a little sick with first unlove, unmoved
by the rich seaweed that slipped into steely water

full of brittle stars, sea anemones; a menagerie
of creatures with Latin names she could still recite,

held sugar kelp across her arms like amber silk,
a gift for me that I wasn't ready to wear. Bending

over, she wanted me to love her sweep of salty
exotica, from metal to opal to white at our feet –

Now, I want to go back, draped in sea-green,
arrange the sea aster, thrift, campion in her hair,

let her take all afternoon to lift each shell and tell
me its story, turn a mussel over to see an oil slick

of blue, its shape like a whale that swallows us
whole, call the strong tide of that place our own.

Poyekhali!

(Let's Go!)

After Public Service Broadcasting's 'Gagarin'

Vostok 1 is Yuri's little lunchbox,
        his spacesuit a scrunched up
smidge of tinfoil. Lid on tight, he is
        a happy crumb of a human being
tumbling about, so forward rolls

look easy up here. Just outside,
        the giant cheese-moon is full and
smiling, and has picked Yuri first
        for her team. He knows when
he gets home the world will chant

'Yuri' like a skipping rhyme –
        108 minutes of doggy paddle across
the shallow end of the universe, tides
        of space-time to jump. Yuri feels
the same froth of excitement now, as when

his rocket launched, powered by love
        and fizzy lemonade. Far below, earth
is a marble in his pocket for playtime,
        a note the shape of Russia from Yuri's mum
gives him permission to dance all day,

        the right way, anyway, upside down.

My daughter's first eye test

Colour of moth wing, faithful against a crush

of darkness, pupils dilated to harvest moons,

left eye struggling for the right, reaching

to peg words on a flapping washing line,

WV turned inside out, OQ made of restless

fuzzy felt, shapes of words humming

like saffron fireflies

flitting far

away

Moving out

Bookshelves swayed,

sagged like the apple trees

we should have pruned

years ago, pages awkward

with dust, my name written

inside front covers in someone

else's handwriting, unread

endings further than roots

that never stopped whispering

to wet earth. Twigs of dried

masking tape still stuck out

of the corner I couldn't

reach, paint cans crept

with rust, *heritage* hardened

to arthritic leaves.

I don't know

when the walls grew wild

with bloom, slow months'

yellowing silence, tiptoeing

past lost keys, chipped cups,

holding my breath against

trip wires of water that

stuttered, spilled from tired

cracks. I slept inside an old

piano riddled with

tiny explosives, dreamt

of crawling out,

the whole house

erupting behind me,

a cadence of

bones

                                        feather

ink.

Acknowledgments:

The quotations come from the collection *Morning in the Burned House* by Margaret Atwood
Huge gratitude to the editors of the journals, magazines and anthologies who were kind enough to read and publish some of these poems:
Beyond the Storm Anthology, Butcher's Dog, Dodging the Rain, Magma, Not Very Quiet press, Strix, The Selkie
Thanks to the judges and organisers of the following competitions: *BBC Proms Poetry competition* and *Poetry on Loan*

Thank you
To Colin Bancroft, for bringing *Nine Pens Press* into existence and for seeing something in this collection of strange specimens worthy of publication. To the inspiring poets in the Zellig group, who have given many of these poems their time and expert consideration. To Lucy Tiller for her continued support, combined with a strong sense of irony. To Max Nichols for his creativity with photography and design. To Neil Slevin, who I value as both editor and friend.

I owe a debt of gratitude to all my friends and family that I know I will never be able to repay.